SCHIRMER'S LIBRARY
OF MUSICAL CLASSICS

Johann Sebastian Bach

Concertos
For the Violin
With Piano Accompaniment

Volume 1111

Concerto in E major

(Arranged and Fingered by Eduard Herrmann)

Volume 1401

→ **Concerto in A minor**

(Arranged and Fingered by Eduard Herrmann)

Volume 1601

Concerto in G minor

(Transcribed by Tivadar Nachèz)

G. SCHIRMER, Inc.

DISTRIBUTED BY
HAL•LEONARD®
CORPORATION
7777 W BLUEMOUND RD PO BOX 13819 MILWAUKEE, WI 53213

Johann Sebastian Bach
(1685-1750)

Concerto I°

Arranged and fingered by
Eduard Herrmann

Allegro moderato

Violin

Piano

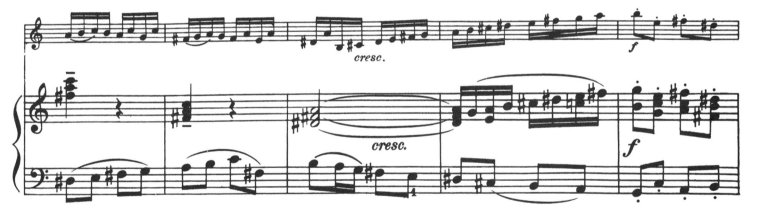

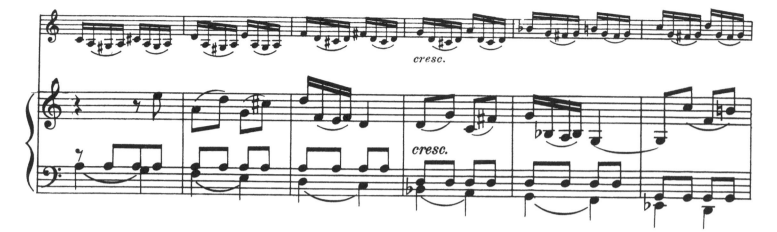

Andante

Allegro assai

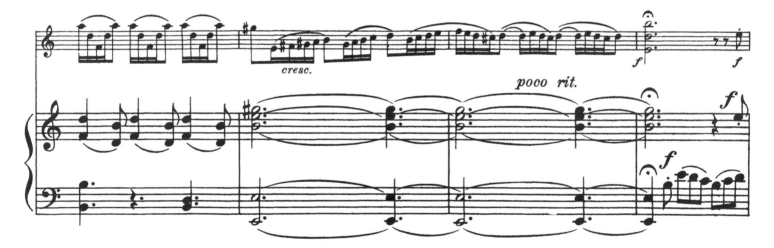

Violin

SCHIRMER'S LIBRARY
OF MUSICAL CLASSICS

Johann Sebastian Bach

Concertos
For the Violin
With Piano Accompaniment

Volume 1111

Concerto in E major

(Arranged and Fingered by Eduard Herrmann)

Volume 1401

→ Concerto in A minor

(Arranged and Fingered by Eduard Herrmann)

Volume 1601

Concerto in G minor

(Transcribed by Tivadar Nachèz)

G. SCHIRMER, Inc.

DISTRIBUTED BY

HAL•LEONARD®
CORPORATION
7777 W BLUEMOUND RD P O BOX 13819 MILWAUKEE, WI 53213

Johann Sebastian Bach

(1685-1750)

Concerto I°

Violin

Arranged and fingered by
Eduard Herrmann

Allegro moderato

Andante

Allegro assai